The WEST Today

PICTURE CREDITS
Cover (back) William Whitehurst/Corbis; cover Charles O'Rear/Corbis; page 1 Carl & Ann Purcell/Corbis; pages 2–3 Richard Hamilton Smith/Corbis; page 4 Mitchell Gerber/Corbis; page 5 (top) Kevin R. Morris/Corbis; pages 5 (middle), 19, 21 Michael Maslan Historic Photographs/Corbis; page 5 (bottom) Ron Watts/Corbis; page 6 Sheldon Collins/Corbis; page 7 Joseph Sohm; Visions of America/Corbis; page 8 (top) Wolfgang Kaehler/Corbis; page 8 (bottom) Robert Holmes/Corbis; page 9 (top) Lake County Museum/Corbis; pages 9 (bottom), 20 Phil Schermeister/Corbis; pages 10 (bottom), 13 Tom Bean/Corbis; pages 10–11 courtesy the Page Museum at the La Brea Tar Pits; page 11 Ted Soqui/Corbis Sygma; page 12 (left) Photodisc; page 12 (right) James L. Amos/Corbis; page 14 Close Murray/Corbis Sygma; page 15 (top) A. Morrison/Corbis Sygma; page15 (bottom) Underwood & Underwood/Corbis; page 16 Corbis Sygma; pages 16–17 Photofest; page 18 (left) Lucka Babini/Corbis; page 18 (top) courtesy Nancy Thurston; page 19 (top) Royalty-Free/Corbis; page 19 (middle) Ann & Peter Bosted; page 19 (bottom) Steve Starr/Corbis; page 21 (top) courtesy Mollie Kathleen Gold Mine, Cripple Creek, Colorado; page 21 (bottom) Royalty-Free/Corbis; page 25 M.L. Sinibaldi/Corbis; page 26–27 Mike Zens/Corbis; pages 27 (bottom), 29, 30 (top and bottom) Michael S. Yamashita/Corbis; page 28 Corbis; page 31 (top) Dan Lamont/Corbis; page 32 (top) David Muench/Corbis; page 32 (middle right) Rick Gayle/Corbis; page 32 (bottom) Ohana Helicopter Tours; page 32 (bottom left) Douglas Peebles/Corbis.

cover: Redwood Forest, California
page 1: cable car
pages 2–3: San Francisco

Produced through the worldwide resources of the National Geographic Society, John M. Fahey, Jr., President and Chief Executive Officer; Gilbert M. Grosvenor, Chairman of the Board; Nina D. Hoffman, Executive Vice President and President, Books and Education Publishing Group.

PREPARED BY NATIONAL GEOGRAPHIC SCHOOL PUBLISHING
Ericka Markman, Senior Vice President and President, Children's Books and Education Publishing Group; Steve Mico, Senior Vice President, Publisher, Editorial Director; Marianne Hiland, Executive Editor; Anita Schwartz, Project Editor; Jim Hiscott, Design Manager; Kristin Hanneman, Illustrations Manager; Diana Bourdrez, Picture Editor; Matt Wascavage, Manager of Publishing Services; Sean Philpotts, Production Manager.

MANUFACTURING AND QUALITY MANAGEMENT
Christopher A. Liedel, Chief Financial Officer; Phillip L. Schlosser, Director; Clifton M. Brown III, Manager.

ART DIRECTION Dan Banks, Project Design Company

PROGRAM DEVELOPMENT Gare Thompson Associates, Inc.

CONSULTANTS/REVIEWERS
Dr. Margit E. McGuire, School of Education, Seattle University, Seattle, Washington

BOOK DEVELOPMENT Nieman Inc.

BOOK DESIGN Three Communication Design, LLC

Published by the National Geographic Society
1145 17th Street, N.W.
Washington, D.C. 20036-4688

ISBN: 978-0-7922-4536-0
ISBN: 0-7922-4536-9

4 5 6 7 8 9 10 11 19 18 17 16 15 14 13
Printed in the U.S.A.

CONTENTS

THE WEST

Most people have heard of the "Wild West." There's still a lot of wildness out West. That can include everything from the region's wild scenery to the wild special effects of today's Hollywood movies.

To learn the answers to the following questions—and other interesting things about the West—read on.

ALASKA

WASHINGTON

OREGON

CALIFORNIA

NEVADA

MILES
0   50   100

0   75 150
KILOMETERS

HAWAII

What's an animatron?
Find out on page 16.

What do you call someone who **parachutes** into a **forest fire**?

Find out on page 26.

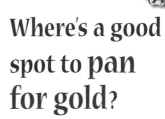

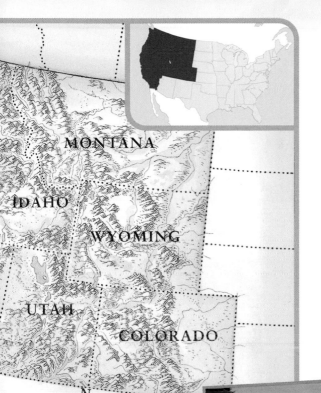

MONTANA

IDAHO

WYOMING

UTAH

COLORADO

N

W E

S

Where's a good spot to **pan for gold**?

Find out on page 19.

Where is the "**crookedest street** in the world"?

Find out on page 9.

TOURING THE WEST

By Lisa Moran

Here are two places in the West you might enjoy visiting. The first is Yellowstone National Park, the world's oldest national park. The second place is San Francisco, one of America's most exciting cities.

Lower Yellowstone Falls

Yellowstone National Park

Yellowstone National Park covers more than two million acres in the northwest corner of Wyoming. Yellowstone is a special place for more than just its size. It was established in 1872. This makes Yellowstone the oldest national park in the world. Most important, Yellowstone is home to natural wonders and fascinating wildlife.

Most visitors to Yellowstone want to get a look at Old Faithful, the world's most famous geyser. A geyser is a natural hot spring that shoots out steam and boiling water. About every 80 minutes, Old Faithful's plume of steam gushes 180 feet into the air!

Yellowstone is home to herds of elk and buffalo. Buffalo are the largest animals in the park. Adults can grow as big as 2,500 pounds. Both black and grizzly bears also live in Yellowstone. Since the bears roam free, visitors to the park often meet them. Remember, a surprised bear can be a dangerous bear! If you hike in Yellowstone, go with a group and make lots of noise. You may even want to wear "bear bells" around your ankles. This way the bears know you're coming!

Visitors watching Old Faithful erupt

Golden Gate Bridge in the fog

Giant cable-winding wheels at Cable Car Museum

City by the Bay

San Francisco, California, lies on a tip of land between the Pacific Ocean and San Francisco Bay. There is water on three sides of "the city by the bay." San Francisco also has many steep hills. Stand on the top of one, and you can see for miles. You better hope it's a clear day, because San Francisco gets a *lot* of fog!

There's an easy and fun way to get around San Francisco's big hills—cable cars. First installed in 1873, San Francisco's cable cars are the only *moving* national landmarks in America. The cable cars are pulled up and down San Francisco's hills by big cables, or wire ropes, turning on huge wheels.

Ride a cable car to the top of Nob Hill and you can visit the Cable Car Museum. There are antique cable cars and the giant cable-winding wheels. These keep the cars traveling at nine and a half miles an hour all the time. You will have to get off the cable car to take a walk down Lombard Street, the "crookedest street in the world." Lombard Street makes eight hairpin turns as it goes down Russian Hill.

The Golden Gate Bridge is a San Francisco landmark. The two-mile-long bridge took four years to build and was finished in 1937. You can walk across the Golden Gate Bridge and get spectacular views of the city—unless there's too much fog.

Exploratorium

San Francisco's Exploratorium is a hands-on science museum with more than 600 exhibits. One of the museum's most famous exhibits is strictly "hands-on." It's called the Tactile Dome. *Tactile* (TAK–tuhl) means "felt by the sense of touch." Visitors to this exhibit make their way through a totally dark maze using only their sense of touch. There are all kinds of weird and wonderful textures to feel—in the dark!

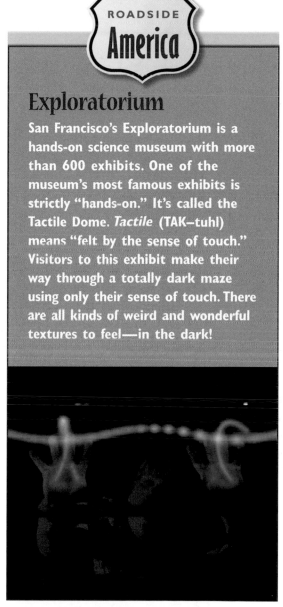

Visitor learning about light waves at the Exploratorium

Saber-Tooths and Dinosaurs

By Matthew Paul

Want a glimpse of the *really* old, *really* wild West? About 40,000 years ago, giant beasts roamed what is now southern California. These included elephant-like mammoths and mastodons, ground sloths that stood over six feet tall, and fierce saber-toothed cats. All these creatures are long gone, but their bones were preserved in the La Brea Tar Pits in Los Angeles, California.

The La Brea Tar Pits are pools formed by sticky oil oozing up out of the ground. For thousands of years, thirsty animals were drawn to the black pools. Thinking the shiny surface was water, they became trapped in the tar. Meat-eating animals would attack them and become trapped themselves. The bones of all these animals were preserved in the tar.

Condor (top left), saber-toothed cats (bottom left), and giant ground sloths (right) at the La Brea Tar Pits long ago

Taking fossils from the La Brea Tar Pits

In the early 1900s, scientists began studying these **fossils** taken from the La Brea Tar Pits. Fossils are the remains of animals and plants that lived long ago. Since then, scientists have identified the fossils of more than 660 different animals and plants here. These fossils have helped scientists put together a picture of what life was like in the West between 40,000 and 8,000 years ago.

Today, you can watch researchers digging fossils out of the La Brea Tar Pits and cleaning them. The fossils are displayed at the George C. Page Museum, which is located at the site.

A Real Jurassic Park

Between 1909 and 1924, a scientist named Earl Douglass found thousands of dinosaur fossils at a site in northeastern Utah. It was no accident that there were so many fossils in this one area. Long ago, a river ran through the sandy soil here. The water attracted dinosaurs. After they died, the river covered their bodies with layers of **sediment** whenever it flooded. Sediment is mud and sand that is carried and deposited by water. Over millions of years, the sediment became rock, preserving the fossils within it. Movements of the Earth's crust carried these rocks to the surface. There, wind and water **erosion** exposed the fossils to sharp-eyed hunters, such as Earl Douglass.

In 1915, President Woodrow Wilson created Dinosaur National Monument. It covers a large area in northeastern Utah and northwestern Colorado. Dinosaur National Monument has some of the largest finds of **Jurassic Period** dinosaur fossils in the world. The Jurassic Period lasted from 208 million to 144 million years ago. Remains of 11 different kinds of Jurassic dinosaurs have been found there. Some of the largest dinosaurs ever, such as the huge plant-eater diplodocus (dih–PLOD–uh–kus), once roamed the area.

Today, Dinosaur National Monument offers many attractions. One is the Dinosaur Quarry, a site that contains about 1,500 fossils. You can visit the Quarry and watch researchers chip fossils from the rock.

Digging fossils at Dinosaur National Monument

Words for You

erosion the slow wearing away of rock caused by water and wind

fossils the remains of animals and plants that lived long ago

Jurassic Period the age in Earth's history from 208 to 144 million years ago

sediment the mud and sand that is carried and deposited by water

Green River, Dinosaur
National Monument

Is That BLOOD or CHOCOLATE SYRUP?

By Anna Keo

A T-Rex looking for a snack sizes up a car. So what if these dinosaurs have been gone for 65 million years? Movie special effects can make almost anything happen.

Yesterday's Special Effects

Special effects create a sense of reality on-screen. Some special effects are simple. Filmmakers use chocolate syrup instead of dripping blood. They place actors inside of monster suits. They use miniature buildings to make their monsters look huge.

Special effects have been used since the earliest days of film. Some special-effects tools were borrowed from the theater. One of these is the flying rig. This is a system of pulleys and a harness that lets an actor appear to fly.

Another tool that filmmakers have long used is matte painting. A matte painting is a detailed painting on glass that provides a background for a filmed scene.

Another tool is stop-action photography. Stop-action photography means filming one frame of film, then stopping, moving an object in the scene, filming another frame, stopping, moving the object again, and so on.

(top) Filmmaker Ray Harryhausen famous for stop-action special effects
(bottom) Special effect from the 1957 movie *The Incredible Shrinking Man*

15

Today's Special Effects

Today's filmmakers have much fancier special-effects tools—and they keep developing more. One tool used often is the blue screen. This is a screen that appears invisible to the camera. An actor is filmed against this screen. Then, the actor's image can be used with any other background, such as the top of a skyscraper.

If an actor needs to get shot or stabbed, the director doesn't smear him with chocolate syrup. Instead, filmmakers use squibs. Squibs are small plastic bags filled with fake blood to produce lifelike wounds.

Another tool is the animatron, a puppet that is moved by remote controls. Animatronics can be used to create realistic monsters and aliens.

The most important new special-effects tool is the computer. Computer-generated images have allowed filmmakers to create whole new worlds.

How Do They Do That?

Here's how filmmakers create some common special effects:

floods Large tanks of water are suddenly dumped onto miniature sets.

exploding car Exploding charges are placed inside a super-lightweight car and set off using remote controls.

actors flying through space An actor is filmed in front of a blue screen. The blue background is removed and the actor's image is placed against a background of space.

violent storms Wind machines, fog machines, and rain cranes provide the nasty elements.

scenes of mass destruction Small models of buildings, trains, and towns are destroyed.

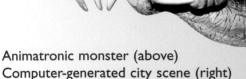

Animatronic monster (above)
Computer-generated city scene (right)

Stunt People

One group of special-effects experts that has been in movies for a long time is the stunt people. These are the actors who perform dangerous or athletic tricks. Stunt people are not the stars, but many films couldn't be done without them. "You don't know our faces or our names," says stunt woman Nancy Thurston. When Nancy began her career, the field had few women. "I always wanted to be a jockey or do stunts," she says. Desk work did not interest her.

Nancy's specialty is the high fall. This seems logical, given her training as a gymnast and high diver. One of her first jobs was a 93-foot fall. An air bag cushioned her landing.

Nancy does more than just falls, however. "You never do the same thing twice," she says. TV shows and movies today have so many different types of stunts. "Someone's always crashing through a wall or window," she says. That should keep her busy.

Go for the Gold!

By Gare Thompson

Do you have gold fever? Do you dream of finding gold and striking it rich? Today, there are many spots in the West where you can still try your hand at prospecting for gold. Along the way, you can learn a lot about the history of mining in the Old West.

Gold and gemstones are still present in old mines.

You might visit Colorado on your quest for gold. You would be following the prospectors who first searched for gold there. Hundreds joined a gold rush to Colorado in 1858. They all thought that they would strike it rich. Most did not. They soon tired of finding only a few gold nuggets or nothing at all. Many left and joined the next gold rush.

These early prospectors looked for gold by sifting the earth by hand. Some used a handmade screen to pan for gold in streams and rivers. They hoped to find nuggets or at least gold dust. Most just found useless rocks.

A few lucky ones found veins, or rich deposits of gold. These prospectors dug mines to get at the gold.

Panning for gold

Now, people try to find gold for fun. One place they go is the Argo Mill in Idaho Springs, Colorado. This is a mining museum. You can see exhibits on what it was like for those early prospectors to search for gold. You can go into a mine and try to find gold in a vein. Remember to use safety gear in a mine. This includes a hard hat, safety glasses, and steel-toed boots or shoes.

You can also pan for gold in a stream. Take your pan and start panning. A good place to look is near rocks. The water moves slowly here. Gold dust is heavier than dirt so it sinks to the bottom of the pan. Be careful as you swirl the water around in your pan. You don't want to lose any gold dust.

So, do you think that you will strike it rich? Well, you probably won't. Hunting for gold is fun. It cures gold fever!

(top right) Mine tour (right) Argo Mill in Colorado

The Legend of Crater Lake

By Katherine Sallé

Long ago, a vast forest covered the Northwest of what is now the United States. A jagged range of snow-covered mountains towered above the forest. Mount Mazama was the tallest peak. The only mountain that came close to its height was Mount Shasta, about one hundred miles away.

The Klamaths are a Native American people. Long ago, they lived in the valley at the base of Mount Mazama. An old Klamath tale tells that Llao, the underworld god, lived in Mount Mazama. Llao's bitter enemy was the sky god, Skell. The Klamaths believed Skell lived in Mount Shasta.

22

Skell and Llao each thought that he was bigger, stronger, and wiser than the other god. Each wanted to defeat the other and rule the world all by himself. Llao and Skell roared at each other for thousands of years. Thunderstorms and earthquakes often interrupted the peace and quiet of the Klamaths' lives.

The two gods agreed to wage one final battle to decide who would rule the world. Llao and Skell each dug a deep pit in the top of his mountain.

Then, each god cut down three thousand trees. Llao rubbed together two sharp stones from the underworld. Flash! A spark lit a blazing fire in his pit. Skell unleashed a spark of lightning from the sky. Flash! The trees in his pit burst into flame.

As darkness fell over the valley, the Klamaths saw flames shooting from the top of Mount Mazama. One hundred miles away, flames were also shooting from the top of Mount Shasta.

The Final Battle

Llao started the battle. He reached into his fire and hurled hot ashes at Skell. Skell reached into his fire and threw **lava**, or hot, melted rock, at Llao. Llao rolled burning trees down the slopes of Mount Mazama. Skell flung back hot, jagged rocks.

The battle raged for two whole weeks. The sky turned black with ash, and the valley was buried in red-hot lava. Finally, a huge rock slammed Llao right in the chest. He toppled over backwards into the fiery pit.

The mountaintop caved in, swallowing Llao in sizzling lava and ash. He was never seen again. Over on Mount Shasta, Skell claimed victory. He put out his fire and filled in the pit to form a new peak for Mount Shasta. Then, he went off to rule the world all by himself.

From that day on, Mount Mazama never regained its pointed peak. Over time, the caved-in pit became round, like a bowl. Thousands of years passed. Snow and rain fell into the bowl, filling it up with the purest, clearest, and bluest water ever seen on Earth. Today, we call it Crater Lake.

Crater Lake is 1,932 feet deep.

Crater Lake Today

Mount Mazama is a **volcano**, a mountain formed by melted rock thrown up from the Earth's crust. A volcano has a **crater**, or hollow, in its mouth. Most volcanoes are shaped like cones. More than 6,000 years ago, Mount Mazama **erupted**, or threw out lava and ash. Its cone collapsed, and the crater filled with rain and melting snow. Today, it is Crater Lake, the deepest lake in the United States.

Crater Lake is in Oregon, about 250 miles south of Portland. Fragments of ancient Mount Mazama form its walls. In 1902, Congress created Crater Lake National Park. Visitors to the park are often surprised to see how clear the water is. People claim you can read a book placed six feet below its surface!

Words for You

crater a hollow in the mouth of a volcano

erupt (by a volcano) throw out lava and ash

lava hot, melted rock flowing from a volcano

volcano a mountain formed by melted rock thrown up from the Earth's crust

SMOKE JUMPERS

By Liz West

In fighting fires, speed is of the greatest importance. City firefighters use trucks to reach fires quickly. Even in wilderness areas, many fires can be reached by road or helicopter. However, sometimes forest fires break out in very remote areas. That is when smoke jumpers are used.

Smoke jumpers are firefighters who specialize in parachuting to fires in hard-to-reach areas. Using fast planes and specially designed parachutes, smoke jumpers can get to fires that are difficult to reach in any other way.

The idea of using planes to fight forest fires started in 1918. At that time, the U.S. Forestry Service just wanted the planes to spot fires in the huge western forests. Once spotted, fires would be fought on foot. Later, planes began dropping cargo to ground crews. It was a short leap from there to the idea of dropping the firefighters themselves.

Some people had a hard time getting used to the idea of airborne firefighters. The main reason was a distrust of people who use parachutes. A Montana regional forester summed up this view. All of them, he felt, are "more or less crazy. Otherwise, they wouldn't be engaged in such a hazardous undertaking."

The First Smoke Jumpers

The idea of airborne firefighters did not go away, but people still feared the risks. So, tests were run. First, human-size dummies and then people were parachuted into the woods. Then, in 1940, the program officially started.

For many jumpers, their training jump was their first plane ride. They got some bumps and bruises upon landing, but they also got the go-ahead. On July 12, smoke jumpers leapt into their first forest fire.

Smoke jumpers do not just try to put out fires. They try to rob them of fuel. Think about it—in the woods, fuel is everywhere. To starve fires, the firefighters use several approaches. On small ground fires, they may dig fire trenches, or firelines. These are areas that are cleared of materials that can catch fire. Brush, trees, dry grass, and shrubs are removed. Firelines surround fires and often keep them from spreading. Sometimes, however, winds can push fires over the fireline.

An early smoke jumper

When fires jump the line, they find fresh fuel. They can spread rapidly. In the worst case, they blow up into firestorms. These are the most dangerous forest fires of all. Firestorms roar like freight trains and grow so hot that sap boils and trees explode.

Luckily, modern smoke jumpers get help from technology. Computer programs often predict what a fire is likely to do. Satellites, weather stations, and lightning detectors help identify small fires before they grow. Airpower helps put out blazes. Planes drop fire-killing chemicals. Helicopters scoop up water from nearby lakes and dump it on flames. Still, the humans are the most important element.

Forest Fire Lingo

The men and women who fight forest fires have special terms for different types of fires:

backfire a second fire that is set on purpose to control the main fire

blowup a fire that suddenly explodes into a huge, disastrous fire

crown fire fire in the tops, or crowns, of trees

gobbler a fire that eats up everything in its path

ground fire a fire that is confined to the ground

reburn a fire that seems to go out but then flares up again

spot fire a small fire that jumps ahead of the main fire

Job Description

Today's smoke jumpers are men and women in their middle twenties. They have already had a few years of firefighting experience. Often, they worked on "hotshot crews," teams of firefighters who drive or hike into the forest.

Smoke jumpers must be in excellent physical shape, since they may have to carry 100-pound packs for miles. They have undergone a tough, five-week training program. They learn how to exit a plane correctly and how to open a parachute. They learn how to maneuver the parachute and how to hit the ground safely.

Trainee smoke jumper learning to use a parachute

Most important of all, they learn to remain calm. Steady nerves are vital for a smoke jumper because every forest fire can become deadly. One 1949 blaze in Mann Gulch, Montana, killed a dozen smoke jumpers.

Smoke jumpers waiting to parachute from a plane

The good news is that such loss of life is rare for smoke jumpers. Usually, their job lasts three days. At that time, the fire is either out or a new group of jumpers takes over. Smoke jumpers never fight fires alone. They go in pairs or small groups. If necessary, more can be called in. At present, there are more than 300 smoke jumpers on call. While surely not crazy, they are definitely a special breed.

Survival and firefighting gear

Tool Kit

Here is some equipment smoke jumpers use:

shovel to bury burning materials

saw to cut down trees and trim branches off them

Pulaski to chop trees and dig fire lines; tool with both ax and hoe blade named for firefighter Edward Pulaski

parachutes to reach fires in remote areas; one main and one emergency chute

let-down rope to get down from a tree if the parachute lands there

hard hat to protect the worker from falling branches and sparks

Insider's Guide

Here are a few more special places that make the West interesting and fun.

Sitka National Historic Park is located in a rain forest in southeast Alaska. Its trails are lined with many striking examples of the totem poles of the Native American peoples of the region.

Are you good at using a yo-yo? The best yo-yo "artists" compete each year at the **National Yo-Yo Contest** in Chico, California.

On the Hawaiian island Kauai, you can get wet at the beach or at **Mt. Waialeale Crater**, the rainiest spot on Earth. The crater receives more than 460 inches of rainfall each year!